Exploring the Internet

Contents

D036600∃

written by John Lockyer

Tasha and her family use their computer every day for all kinds of things, like writing letters and making pictures and charts. But Tasha's favorite thing is exploring the Internet.

She knows that the World Wide Web is a place where people can see cartoons, hear music, read the news, visit libraries and museums, get useful information, and even look out the window of a space shuttle.

The World Wide Web is a like a huge library. It is full of information about almost anything you can think of. You can find out about things that happened yesterday, or last month, or even thousands of years ago.

There is information about people, places, sports, animals, machines, and all kinds of other things. All the information is on web pages or *websites*. The Internet connects computers all over the world like a giant spider's web.

If Tasha wants information about the planets, she uses the Internet to help her. She starts with a *search engine*. Almost anything on the Internet can be found with the help of a search engine.

Tasha types the *keyword* planets into the window of the search engine. Then she moves the cursor onto the *Go* or the *Search* button, and she clicks on the *mouse*.

In a few seconds, the screen shows a list of thousands of different websites about planets. Tasha clicks on a website that looks interesting.

She reads about the earth, the moon, and Mars. Then she clicks on the Back button to go back to the list to choose another website. Tasha goes from one site to another. She is *surfing the net*.

Tasha sees pictures of the planets on the Internet. She finds out which one is the smallest and which one is the largest. She watches a video of a space shuttle landing back on earth, and she even hears the voice of an astronaut.

Tasha finds a lot of interesting information on a website about Mars. She thinks that she might want to learn more about Mars later, so she clicks on the *Favorites* button. Then she clicks on *Add* and saves the Mars website in the Favorites box. Now she can find it easily whenever she wants to look at it again.

Some of the Mars websites have colored words or pictures with a line under them. These are called *hyperlinks*.

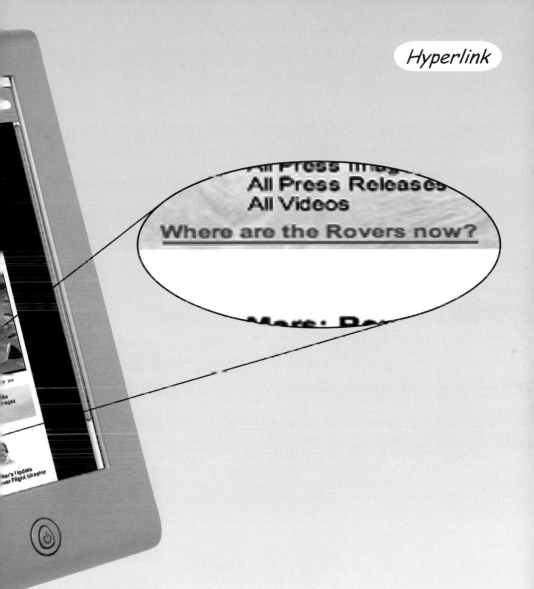

When Tasha points the cursor at a hyperlink, a little hand shows on the screen. If she clicks on a hyperlink, a new page about Mars will open up on the screen.

Tasha looks at the site about Mars that she has saved. She reads about the red rocks and dust storms on Mars, and she looks at pictures of its giant volcano.

Previous   Contents   Next

Schedule for Mars surface excursion.

How a manned spaceship may land on mars and take off to link up with the "mother" ship.

MARS SURFACE EXCURSION

(1) DE-ORBIT

(2) ENTRY

(9) RENDEZVOUS & DOCKING

(3) SHROUD & HEAT SHIELD JETTISON

(8) STAGING

(4) DESCENT BRAKING

(5) LANDING

(6) SURFACE OPERATIONS

(7) ASCENT

She watches a spacecraft driving there. She learns that Mars has its own moons, which look a bit like potatoes! Tasha can learn all about Mars on the wonderful World Wide Web.

When Tasha surfs the net, she can go to all kinds of websites. She can find out information about whatever she wants to know. She can learn many things from the past and the present, and she will have lots of fun.